Learning

Three-Octave Arpeggios

on the Cello

by Cassia Harvey

CHP359

©2019 by C. Harvey Publications All Rights Reserved.

www.learnstrings.com - downloadable books
www.charveypublications.com - print books

Table of Contents, Page One

Section	Page
What Arpeggios Are	4
Why Practice Arpeggios?	5
How This Book Works	5
Shifting Tips for Arpeggios	6

Part One: Arpeggios with Fingering No. 1

C major	8
C minor	11
D-flat major	12
C-sharp minor	15
D major	16
D minor	19
E-flat major	20
E-flat minor	23
E major	24
E minor	27
F major	28
F minor	31
F-sharp major	32
F-sharp minor	35
G major	36
G minor	39
A-flat major	40
G-sharp minor	43
A major	44
A minor	47
B-flat major	48
B-flat minor	51
B major	52
B minor	55

Part Two: Arpeggios with Fingering No. 2

C major	56
C minor	57
D-flat major	58
C-sharp minor	59

©2019 C. Harvey Publications All Rights Reserved.

Learning Three-Octave Arpeggios on the Cello

Table of Contents, Page Two

Section	Page
Part Two: Arpeggios with Fingering No. 2 *cont.*	
D major	60
D minor	61
E-flat major	62
E-flat minor	63
E major	64
E minor	65
F major	66
F minor	67
F-sharp major	68
F-sharp minor	69
G major	70
G minor	71
A-flat major	72
G-sharp minor	73
A major	74
A minor	75
B-flat major	76
B-flat minor	77
B major	78
B minor	79
Arpeggio Fingering No. 2: Major Shifting Exercise	80
Arpeggio Fingering No. 2: Minor Shifting Exercise	81
Part Three: Arpeggios with Fingering No. 3	
C major	82
C minor	84
D-flat major	86
C-sharp minor	88
D major	90
D minor	92
E-flat major	94
E-flat minor	96

©2019 C. Harvey Publications All Rights Reserved.

Table of Contents, Page Three

Section	Page
Part Three: Arpeggios with Fingering No. 3 *cont.*	
E major	98
E minor	100
F major	102
F minor	104
F-sharp major	106
F-sharp minor	108
G major	110
G minor	112
A-flat major	114
G-sharp minor	116
A major	118
A minor	120
B-flat major	122
B-flat minor	124
B major	126
B minor	128
Arpeggio Fingering No. 3: Thumb Study in Major Keys	130
Arpeggio Fingering No. 3: Thumb Study in Minor Keys	131
Part Four: Complete Arpeggios	
Sevcik's Arpeggio Cycle	132
Major and Minor Arpeggios: Fingering No. 1	139
Major and Minor Arpeggios: Fingering No. 2	142
Major and Minor Arpeggios: Fingering No. 3	145

What Arpeggios Are

An arpeggio is a chord with the notes played one after another in order, instead of all at once.

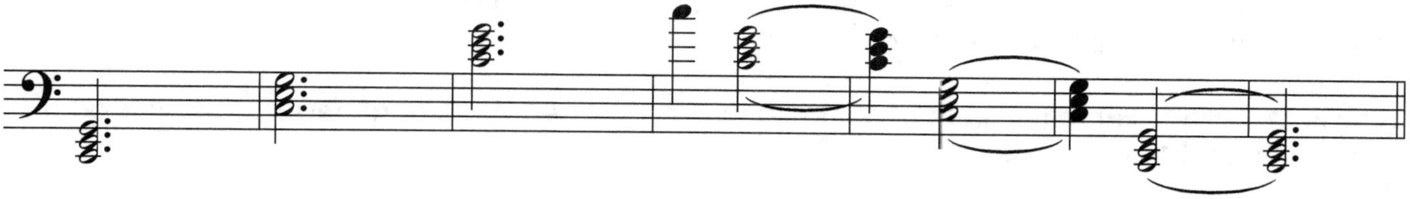

C major arpeggio, based on chords above.

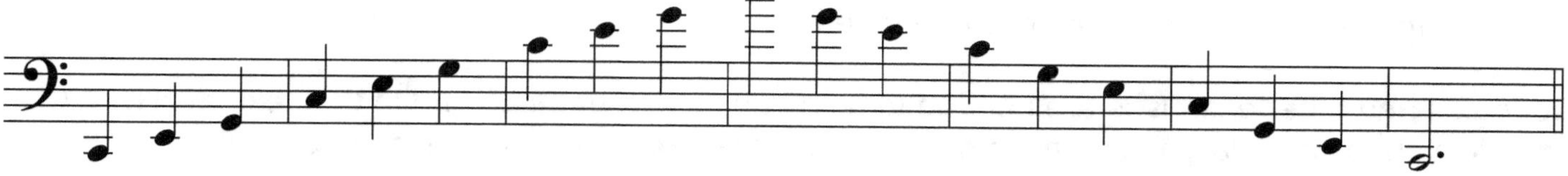

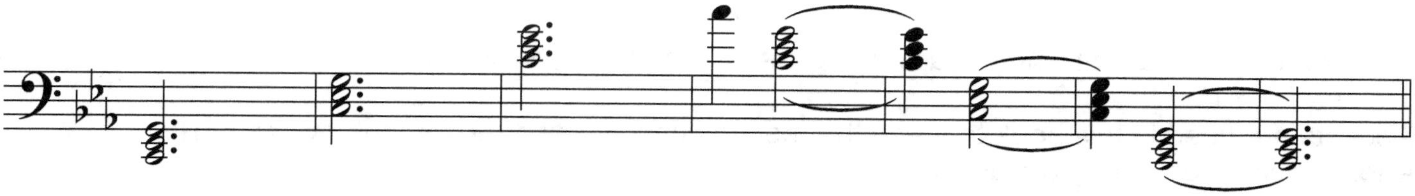

C minor arpeggio, based on chords above.

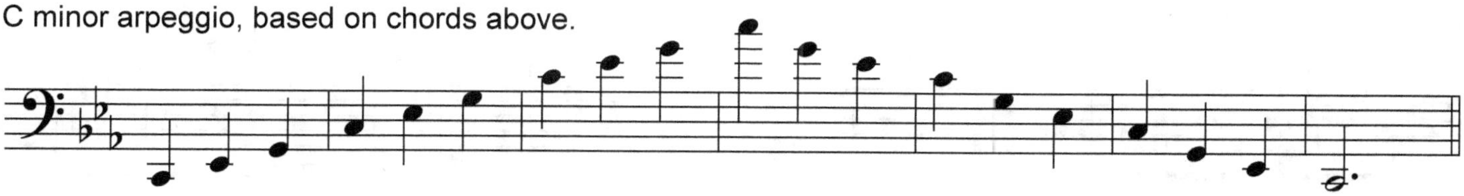

Arpeggios are also related to scales.
Here is the C major scale with the notes of the arpeggio sized bigger than the other notes:

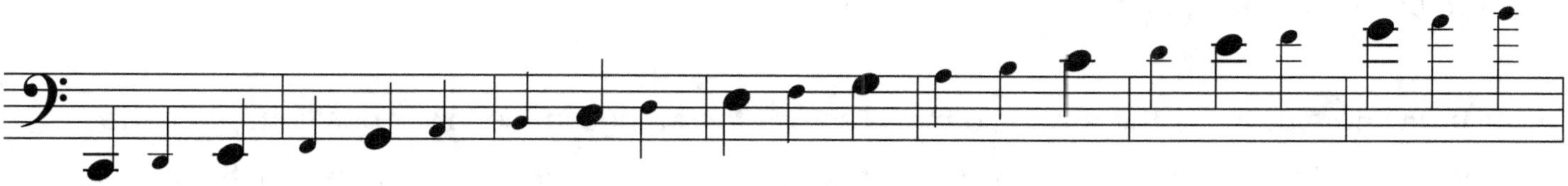

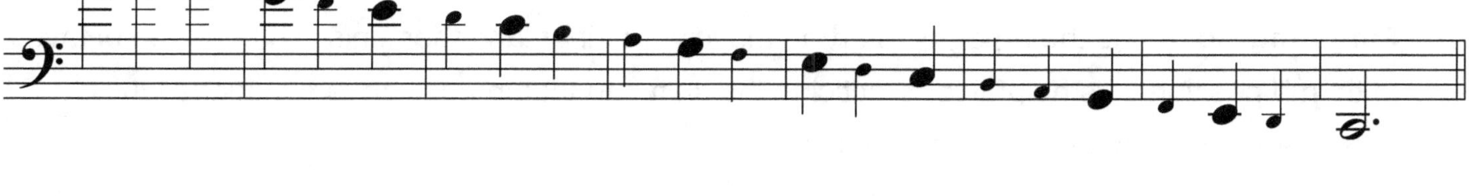

Why Add Arpeggios to Your Practice?

Scales are used to teach notes in order. The spaces and shifts in scales are intervals of a second.

Arpeggios are used to teach notes with larger spaces and shifts between them. The spaces and shifts in arpeggios are intervals of thirds and fourths.

Because the shifts in arpeggios are of a greater distance, **arpeggios are generally considered to be more difficult than scales.**

Although scales are an important building block of cello technique, they are limited in that they only teach shifting between notes that are close together.

Arpeggios and other exercises are needed to help you take your technique to the next level by teaching you to cover larger distances on the cello fingerboard precisely and consistently.

How This Book Works

• Each arpeggio is taught using spacing exercises and shifting exercises.

• Accents are used in this book to teach the mechanical left-hand movement involved in performance-level arpeggio playing.

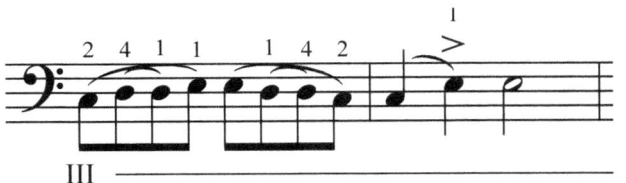 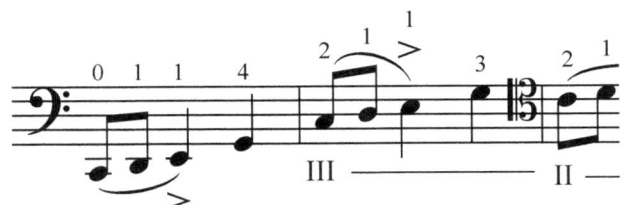

The Three Arpeggio Fingerings

- **Fingering No. 1** goes across strings. It is helpful for teaching spacing up high on the lower strings, as well as general fingerboard geography.

- **Fingering No. 2** has the arpeggio move across the strings in the lower positions, with the majority of high shifting up the A string. It is helpful for learning the geography of the A string and for building confidence in shifting.

- **Fingering No. 3** has the arpeggio start on the lower strings and then finish with the top octave in thumb position. It is helpful for practicing the shift into thumb position, a technique which is otherwise rarely covered in cello technique.

©2019 C. Harvey Publications All Rights Reserved.

Shifting Tips for Arpeggios

- Focus on remembering the physical spaces on the fingerboard and the correct sounds of the arpeggios.
- As you shift, concentrate on the placement of both the starting note and the arrival note to help you learn the distance between the notes.
- Keep your hand relaxed as you shift so that tension does not obscure your sense of distance.
- When you are learning the arpeggios, try to shift at a slow and even speed to help cement muscle memory and your knowledge of the spacing. A slight portamento sound is fine to hear in the exercises but work to remove it in the actual arpeggio.
- Keep your elbow high enough for your hand to move easily over the side of the cello when shifting.
- Shift on the tips of strong, curved fingers. If the shifting finger collapses at all, all of the notes in the arrival position will be compromised.
- Because these arpeggios cover the entire distance of the fingerboard, they require an athletic movement of the left arm. Make sure the arm and elbow move along with the hand and do not lag behind or drag on the hand.

Thumb Placement in Arpeggios

- When playing in the higher positions, the thumb should generally rest gently on the fingerboard across two strings, in the traditional "thumb position."
- In Fingering No. 1, the thumb can be placed on the string when the hand shifts into 6th or 7th position.
- In Fingering No. 2, the thumb can be placed on the string for the top few notes of the arpeggio (or for the top octave of the arpeggio on pages 66-79) to help to stabilize the hand.
- In Fingering No. 3, the thumb is used in the arpeggio fingering itself. Make sure the thumb is placed across both the A and D strings to make the hand as stable as possible at the top of the arpeggio.

Auditioning with Arpeggios: Practical Fingerings to Use

- Fingering No. 1 for C, D-flat, D, E-fat, E, F, and F-sharp major arpeggios
- Fingering No. 1 for C, C-sharp, D, E-flat, E, F, and F-sharp minor arpeggios.
- Fingering No. 2 for G, A-flat, A, B-flat, and B major arpeggios.
- Fingering No. 2 for G, G-sharp, A, B-flat, and B minor arpeggios.

Part One: Fingering No. 1

C Major Arpeggio

Cassia Harvey

Note: In this book, Roman numerals refer to strings:
I = A string, II = D string, III = G string, IV = C string

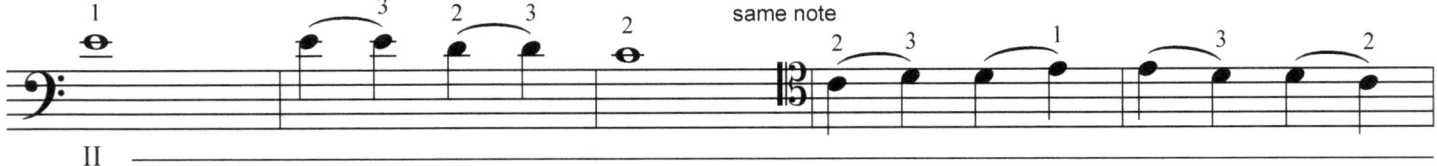

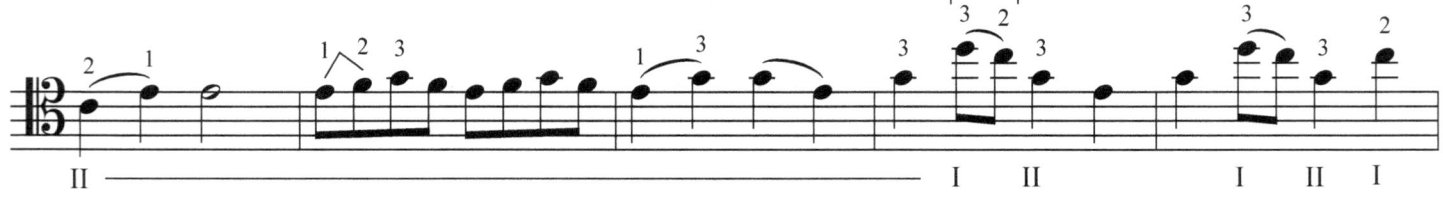

©2019 C. Harvey Publications All Rights Reserved.

Learning the Arpeggio - Part Two

10 C Major Arpeggio, Fingering No. 1   Learning Three-Octave Arpeggios on the Cello

Putting the Arpeggio Together

©2019 C. Harvey Publications All Rights Reserved.

C Minor Arpeggio

D♭ Major Arpeggio

Learning Three-Octave Arpeggios on the Cello — D♭ Major Arpeggio, Fingering No. 1 — 13

Learning the Arpeggio - Part Two

©2019 C. Harvey Publications All Rights Reserved.

14 D♭ Major Arpeggio, Fingering No. 1   Learning Three-Octave Arpeggios on the Cello

Putting the Arpeggio Together

©2019 C. Harvey Publications All Rights Reserved.

C# Minor Arpeggio

D Major Arpeggio

Learning Three-Octave Arpeggios on the Cello — D Major Arpeggio, Fingering No. 1

Learning the Arpeggio - Part Two

©2019 C. Harvey Publications All Rights Reserved.

Putting the Arpeggio Together

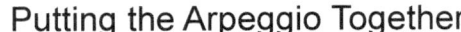

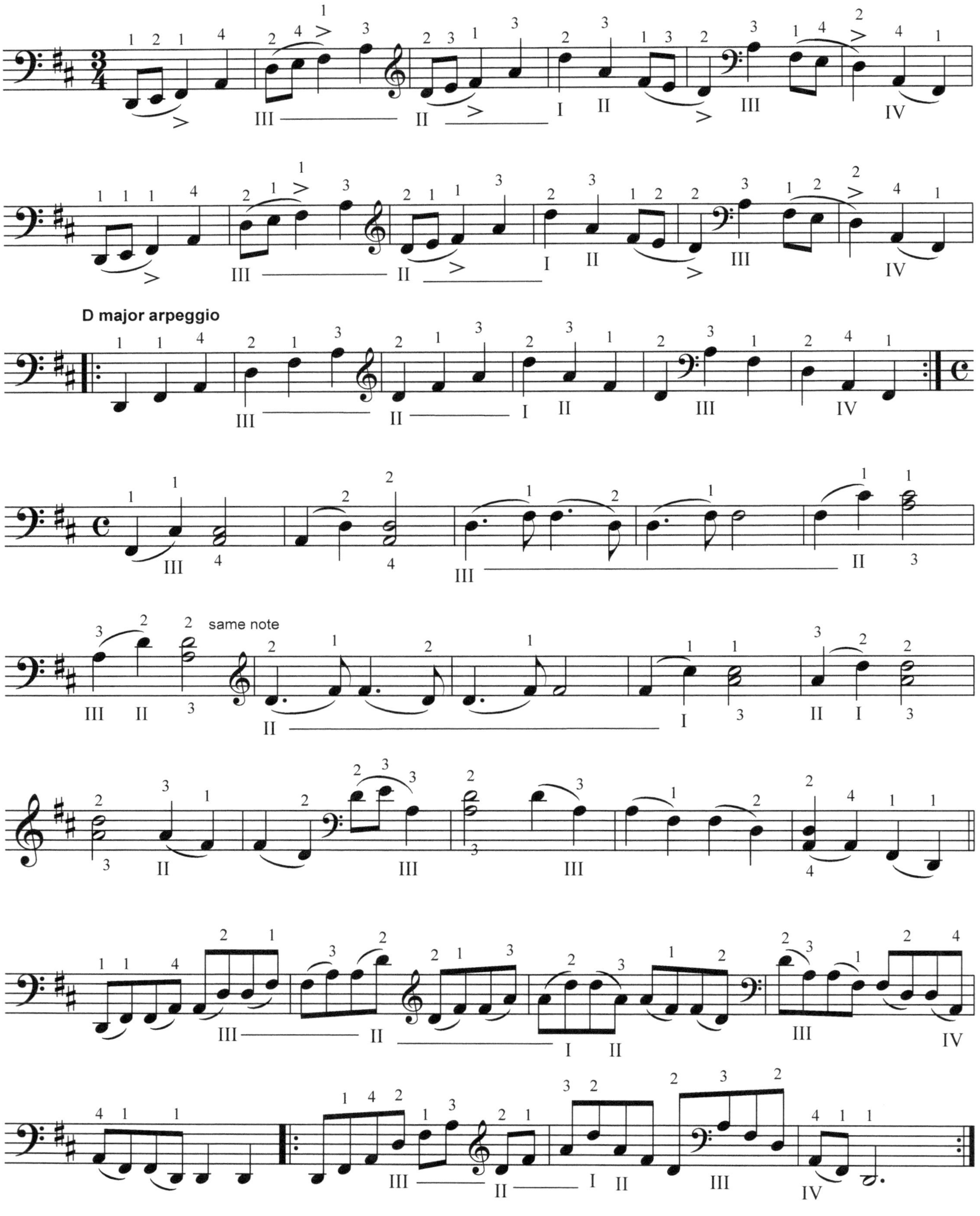

©2019 C. Harvey Publications All Rights Reserved.

D Minor Arpeggio

E♭ Major Arpeggio

Learning Three-Octave Arpeggios on the Cello — E♭ Major Arpeggio, Fingering No. 1

Learning the Arpeggio - Part Two

©2019 C. Harvey Publications All Rights Reserved.

E♭ Major Arpeggio, Fingering No. 1
Learning Three-Octave Arpeggios on the Cello

Putting the Arpeggio Together

©2019 C. Harvey Publications All Rights Reserved.

Learning Three-Octave Arpeggios on the Cello 23

E♭ Minor Arpeggio

E Major Arpeggio

Learning Three-Octave Arpeggios on the Cello — E Major Arpeggio, Fingering No. 1

Learning the Arpeggio - Part Two

©2019 C. Harvey Publications All Rights Reserved.

26 E Major Arpeggio, Fingering No. 1 Learning Three-Octave Arpeggios on the Cello

Putting the Arpeggio Together

©2019 C. Harvey Publications All Rights Reserved.

Learning Three-Octave Arpeggios on the Cello

E Minor Arpeggio

F Major Arpeggio

Learning Three-Octave Arpeggios on the Cello F Major Arpeggio, Fingering No. 1

Learning the Arpeggio - Part Two

F Major Arpeggio, Fingering No. 1

Learning Three-Octave Arpeggios on the Cello

Putting the Arpeggio Together

©2019 C. Harvey Publications All Rights Reserved.

F Minor Arpeggio

F# Major Arpeggio

Learning the Arpeggio - Part Two

F# Major Arpeggio, Fingering No. 1

34 F# Major Arpeggio, Fingering No. 1   Learning Three-Octave Arpeggios on the Cello

Putting the Arpeggio Together

Learning Three-Octave Arpeggios on the Cello

F# Minor Arpeggio

G Major Arpeggio

Learning Three-Octave Arpeggios on the Cello

Note: If you are learning arpeggios for an audition, the fingerings for the G, A♭, A, B♭, and B arpeggios on pages 70-79 would generally be more reliable in a performance situation. The fingerings on pages 36-55 are included mainly to train the hand in the upper positions on the lower strings.

©2019 C. Harvey Publications All Rights Reserved.

Learning Three-Octave Arpeggios on the Cello G Major Arpeggio, Fingering No. 1

Learning the Arpeggio - Part Two

38 G Major Arpeggio, Fingering No. 1   Learning Three-Octave Arpeggios on the Cello

Putting the Arpeggio Together

©2019 C. Harvey Publications All Rights Reserved.

Learning Three-Octave Arpeggios on the Cello

G Minor Arpeggio

A♭ Major Arpeggio

Learning the Arpeggio - Part Two

42 A♭ Major Arpeggio, Fingering No. 1

Putting the Arpeggio Together

A♭ major arpeggio

©2019 C. Harvey Publications All Rights Reserved.

Learning Three-Octave Arpeggios on the Cello

G# Minor Arpeggio

A Major Arpeggio

Learning the Arpeggio - Part Two

46 A Major Arpeggio, Fingering No. 1 Learning Three-Octave Arpeggios on the Cello

Putting the Arpeggio Together

A Minor Arpeggio

B♭ Major Arpeggio

Learning Three-Octave Arpeggios on the Cello — B♭ Major Arpeggio, Fingering No. 1

Learning the Arpeggio - Part Two

B♭ Major Arpeggio, Fingering No. 1

Putting the Arpeggio Together

B♭ Minor Arpeggio

B Major Arpeggio

Learning Three-Octave Arpeggios on the Cello — B Major Arpeggio, Fingering No. 1 — 53

Learning the Arpeggio - Part Two

©2019 C. Harvey Publications All Rights Reserved

54　B Major Arpeggio, Fingering No. 1　　　Learning Three-Octave Arpeggios on the Cello

Putting the Arpeggio Together

B major arpeggio

©2019 C. Harvey Publications All Rights Reserved.

Learning Three-Octave Arpeggios on the Cello

B Minor Arpeggio

Part Two: Fingering No. 2

Note: In Part Two, half steps are marked and whole steps are not. You can assume that a whole step is indicated if no half step is marked.

Learning Three-Octave Arpeggios on the Cello — Fingering No. 2

C Minor Arpeggio

58 Fingering No. 2 — Learning Three-Octave Arpeggios on the Cello

D♭ Major Arpeggio

Learning Three-Octave Arpeggios on the Cello — Fingering No. 2 — 59

C# Minor Arpeggio

©2019 C. Harvey Publications All Rights Reserved.

D Major Arpeggio

Learning Three-Octave Arpeggios on the Cello — Fingering No. 2 — 61

D Minor Arpeggio

62 Fingering No. 2 — Learning Three-Octave Arpeggios on the Cello

E♭ Major Arpeggio

Learning Three-Octave Arpeggios on the Cello — Fingering No. 2 — 63

E♭ Minor Arpeggio

©2019 C. Harvey Publications All Rights Reserved.

64 Fingering No. 2 Learning Three-Octave Arpeggios on the Cello

E Major Arpeggio

Learning Three-Octave Arpeggios on the Cello — Fingering No. 2

E Minor Arpeggio

©2019 C. Harvey Publications All Rights Reserved.

F Major Arpeggio

Learning Three-Octave Arpeggios on the Cello — Fingering No. 2

F Minor Arpeggio

©2019 C. Harvey Publications All Rights Reserved.

Learning Three-Octave Arpeggios on the Cello — Fingering No. 2 — 69

F# Minor Arpeggio

©2019 C. Harvey Publications All Rights Reserved.

G Major Arpeggio

Learning Three-Octave Arpeggios on the Cello Fingering No. 2

G Minor Arpeggio

A♭ Major Arpeggio

Learning Three-Octave Arpeggios on the Cello — Fingering No. 2 — 73

G# Minor Arpeggio

A Major Arpeggio

Learning Three-Octave Arpeggios on the Cello — Fingering No. 2

A Minor Arpeggio

B♭ Major Arpeggio

Learning Three-Octave Arpeggios on the Cello — Fingering No. 2

B♭ Minor Arpeggio

B Major Arpeggio

Learning Three-Octave Arpeggios on the Cello — Fingering No. 2

B Minor Arpeggio

Arpeggio Fingering No. 2: Major Shifting Exercise

Learning Three-Octave Arpeggios on the Cello

Fingering No. 2

Arpeggio Fingering No. 2: Minor Shifting Exercise

82

Part Three: Fingering No. 3

C Major Arpeggio

Learning Three-Octave Arpeggios on the Cello

Fingering No. 3

©2019 C. Harvey Publications All Rights Reserved.

C Minor Arpeggio

Learning Three-Octave Arpeggios on the Cello — Fingering No. 3

C minor arpeggio

86 Fingering No. 3 — Learning Three-Octave Arpeggios on the Cello

D♭ Major Arpeggio

©2019 C. Harvey Publications All Rights Reserved.

Learning Three-Octave Arpeggios on the Cello

Fingering No. 3

D♭ major arpeggio

C# Minor Arpeggio

Learning Three-Octave Arpeggios on the Cello — Fingering No. 3

D Major Arpeggio

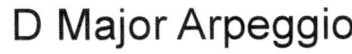

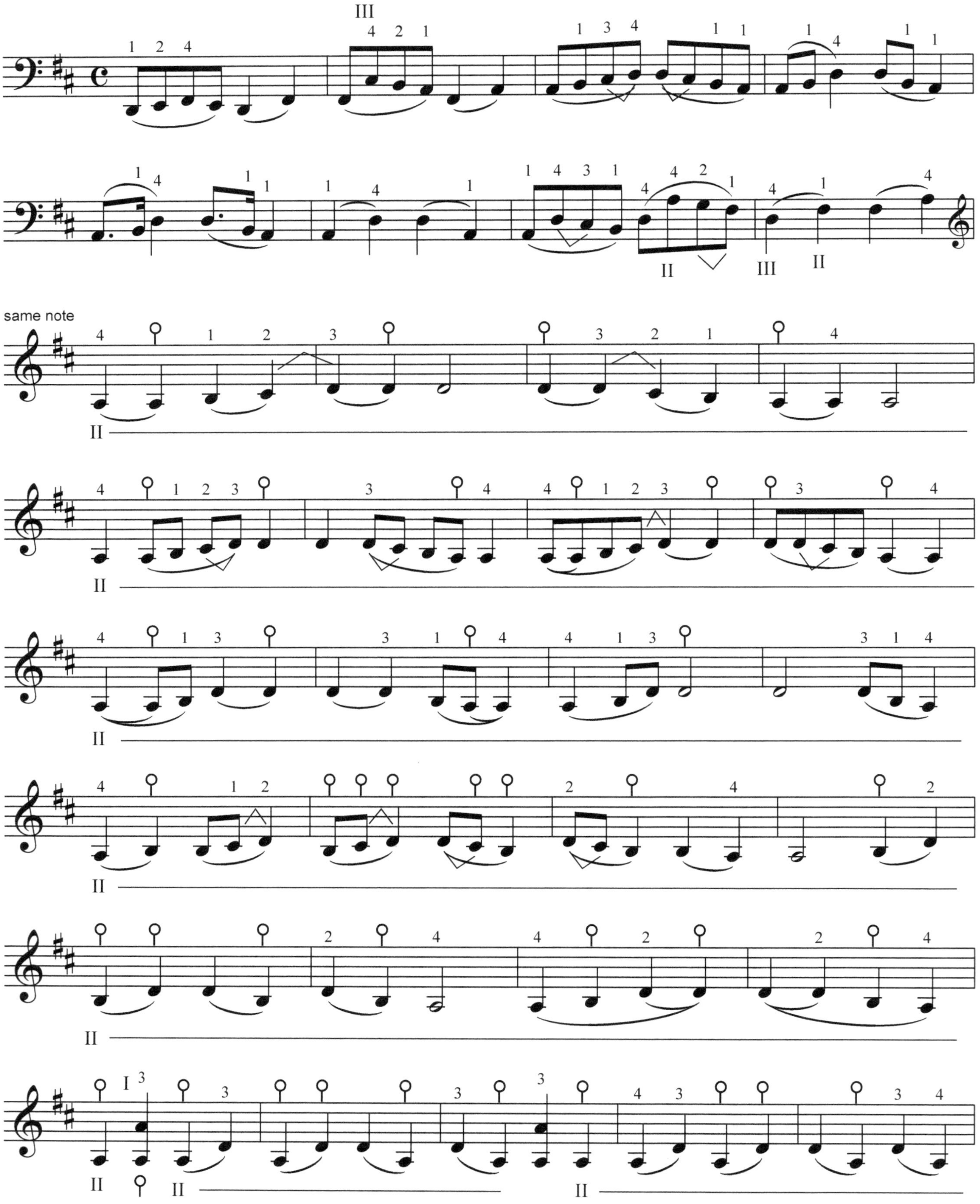

©2019 C. Harvey Publications All Rights Reserved.

Learning Three-Octave Arpeggios on the Cello
Fingering No. 3

D major arpeggio

D Minor Arpeggio

Learning Three-Octave Arpeggios on the Cello

Fingering No. 3

D minor arpeggio

E♭ Major Arpeggio

Learning Three-Octave Arpeggios on the Cello — Fingering No. 3

E♭ Minor Arpeggio

Learning Three-Octave Arpeggios on the Cello — Fingering No. 3

E Major Arpeggio

Learning Three-Octave Arpeggios on the Cello

Fingering No. 3

©2019 C. Harvey Publications All Rights Reserved.

E Minor Arpeggio

Learning Three-Octave Arpeggios on the Cello — Fingering No. 3

F Major Arpeggio

Learning Three-Octave Arpeggios on the Cello   Fingering No. 3   103

F Minor Arpeggio

Learning Three-Octave Arpeggios on the Cello — Fingering No. 3

F minor arpeggio

F# Major Arpeggio

Learning Three-Octave Arpeggios on the Cello — Fingering No. 3

F# Minor Arpeggio

Learning Three-Octave Arpeggios on the Cello — Fingering No. 3

G Major Arpeggio

Learning Three-Octave Arpeggios on the Cello

Fingering No. 3

©2019 C. Harvey Publications All Rights Reserved.

G Minor Arpeggio

Learning Three-Octave Arpeggios on the Cello — Fingering No. 3

A♭ Major Arpeggio

Learning Three-Octave Arpeggios on the Cello
Fingering No. 3

G# Minor Arpeggio

Learning Three-Octave Arpeggios on the Cello — Fingering No. 3

A Major Arpeggio

Learning Three-Octave Arpeggios on the Cello — Fingering No. 3

A Minor Arpeggio

Learning Three-Octave Arpeggios on the Cello — Fingering No. 3

122 Fingering No. 3 Learning Three-Octave Arpeggios on the Cello

B♭ Major Arpeggio

©2019 C. Harvey Publications All Rights Reserved.

Learning Three-Octave Arpeggios on the Cello

Fingering No. 3

124 Fingering No. 3 Learning Three-Octave Arpeggios on the Cello

B♭ Minor Arpeggio

©2019 C. Harvey Publications All Rights Reserved.

Learning Three-Octave Arpeggios on the Cello — Fingering No. 3

B Major Arpeggio

Learning Three-Octave Arpeggios on the Cello — Fingering No. 3 — 127

©2019 C. Harvey Publications All Rights Reserved.

B Minor Arpeggio

Learning Three-Octave Arpeggios on the Cello — Fingering No. 3

Arpeggio Fingering No. 3: Thumb Study in Major Keys

Learning Three-Octave Arpeggios on the Cello — Fingering No. 3 — 131

Arpeggio Fingering No. 3: Thumb Study in Minor Keys

©2019 C. Harvey Publications All Rights Reserved.

Part Four: Complete Arpeggios

Sevcik's Arpeggio Cycle

©2019 C. Harvey Publications All Rights Reserved.

Learning Three-Octave Arpeggios on the Cello   Sevcik's Arpeggio Cycle   133

©2019 C. Harvey Publications All Rights Reserved.

Learning Three-Octave Arpeggios on the Cello
Sevcik's Arpeggio Cycle

Learning Three-Octave Arpeggios on the Cello

Sevcik's Arpeggio Cycle

138 Sevcik's Arpeggio Cycle Learning Three-Octave Arpeggios on the Cello

©2019 C. Harvey Publications All Rights Reserved.

Major and Minor Arpeggios: Fingering No. 1

Learning Three-Octave Arpeggios on the Cello
Major and Minor Arpeggios: Fingering No. 1

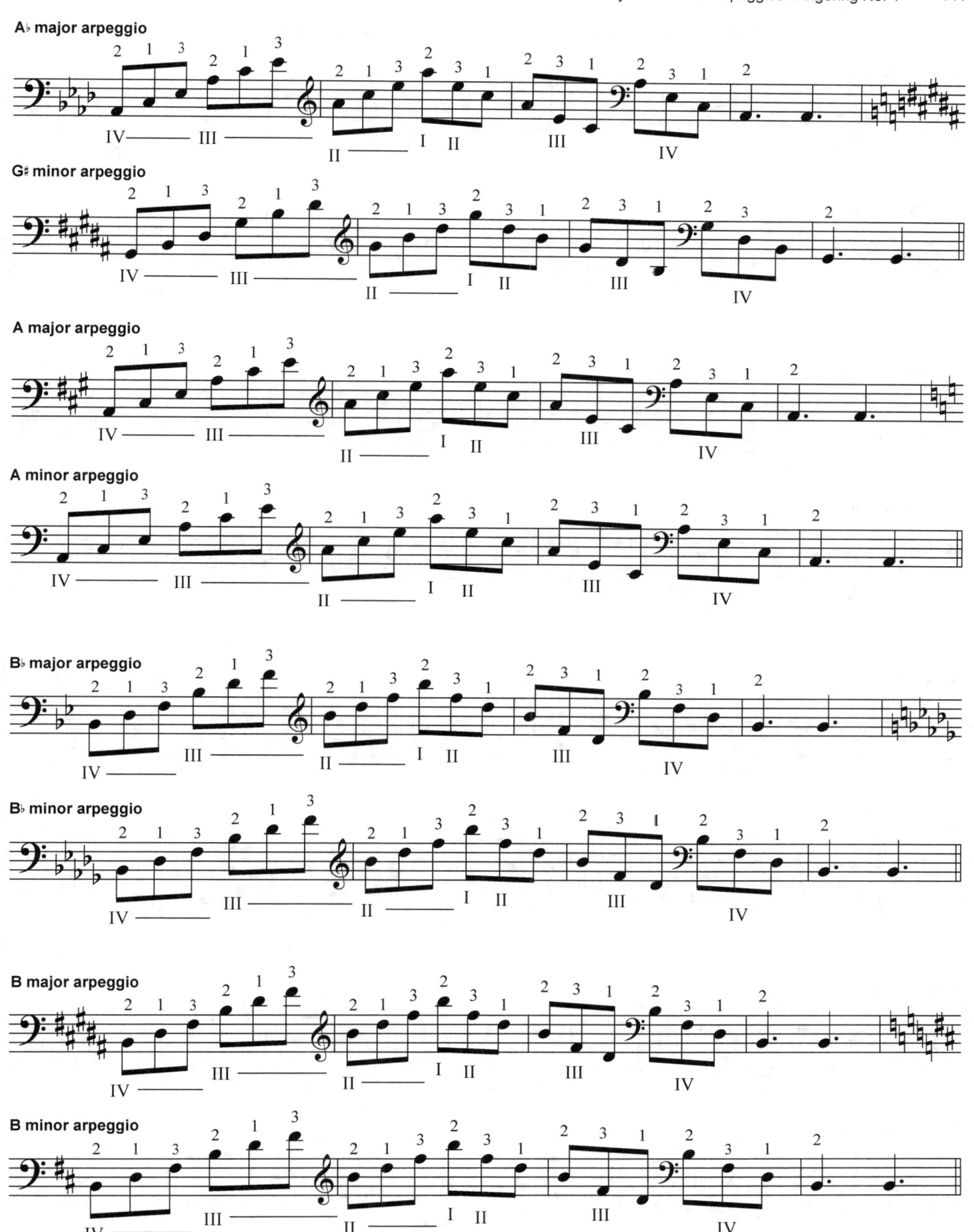

©2019 C. Harvey Publications All Rights Reserved.

Major and Minor Arpeggios: Fingering No. 2

Learning Three-Octave Arpeggios on the Cello — Major and Minor Arpeggios: Fingering No. 2 — 143

©2019 C. Harvey Publications All Rights Reserved.

Learning Three-Octave Arpeggios on the Cello

Major and Minor Arpeggios: Fingering No. 3

©2019 C. Harvey Publications All Rights Reserved.

146 Major and Minor Arpeggios: Fingering No. 3   Learning Three-Octave Arpeggios on the Cello

©2019 C. Harvey Publications All Rights Reserved.

Learning Three-Octave Arpeggios on the Cello — Major and Minor Arpeggios: Fingering No. 3 — 147

©2019 C. Harvey Publications All Rights Reserved.

Also available from www.charveypublications.com:

A book that teaches every note of the first two movements of the Saint-Saens Cello Concerto No. 1.

www.ingramcontent.com/pod-product-compliance
Lightning Source LLC
Chambersburg PA
CBHW051411070526
44584CB00023B/3385